THE PEOPLE MANAGI POCKETBOOK

D1101113

By Ian Fleming
Drawings by Alexis Archier

"Packed with concise information and suggestions. The message is never lost."
Duncan Monroe, Business Planning Executive, Dalgety Food Ingredients.

"This excellent handbook provides particularly useful advice for those difficult personal situations which other textbooks avoid."
Michael Lockhart, Regional Director, English Sports Council.

CONTENTS

MANAGING: WHAT'S DIFFERENT?

ACHIEVING RESULTS

YOU THE MANAGER

DEALING WITH PEOPLE

BUILDING TEAMS

DEVELOPING ABILITIES

INTRODUCTION

This book is intended for people who find themselves in charge of others. The job title may vary. Any training received may well have concentrated on theory: what ought to be done. In reality, things are never that simple.

This book aims to fill the gap by offering pointers to those tricky situations for which nobody is prepared.

Each example is split into three parts:

Signs - that indicate there's a problem
Possible reasons - as to why it could be happening
Then try - practical suggestions to follow

Points to bear in mind

When faced with difficult situations, as far as possible:

- Don't panic; think before you act
- Be clear of the facts; don't act on emotion
- If there are procedures in your organisation, follow them
- Keep a note of what you do; you may need it later
- Don't be afraid to ask for help, either when the situation arises or, afterwards, to talk through what happened

MANAGING: WHAT'S DIFFERENT?

MANAGING: WHAT'S DIFFERENT?

WHAT'S INVOLVED

Moving into a managerial role involves making changes from the way you previously performed.

FROM		TO
'Doing' the job	→	an uncertain 'supervisory' role
Using 'technical skills	→	placing emphasis on people and admin skills
Using well-developed skills	→	having to learn new ones
Being delegated tasks	→	having to delegate to others
Controlling the output	→	being judged on the output and quality of others
Having knowledge	→	managing others, often with more knowledge

● Often people:
  - fail to recognise and understand these differences.
  - are not helped to develop the necessary skills.
  - as a result ..... don't perform in the job.

MANAGING: WHAT'S DIFFERENT?

NEW & NOT ENJOYING IT?
SIGNS

You find yourself:
- Working long hours and taking work home (family complain?)
- Finding it difficult to supervise people who are friends and ex-colleagues
- In a job that holds little satisfaction
- Showing signs of stress:
    - Physical (tired, headaches)
    - Emotional (irritable, tension)
    - Mental (worry, poor decisions)

- Believing that life will be easier once you've mastered the job and you're giving it time .....
- Not being able to talk to anyone - it must be you; everyone else appears to be coping
- Being put to the test by staff (eg: they stand around chatting) ..... how do you handle it?

NEW AND NOT ENJOYING IT?
POSSIBLE REASONS

- Perhaps you are struggling to make the changes needed to do the job? You could be passing through the stages of:

(Shock) — initially finding that the job was not as you had expected

(Denial) — believing that it's not as bad as you had first thought ..... really quite easy?

(Depression) — becoming aware of the need to make changes and the (potential) problems this could cause

(Accepting reality) — recognising that you need to start to do something different

(Testing) — trying new ways and watching peoples' reactions

(Searching for meaning) — understanding what these changes mean for you and the way you operate

(Acceptance) — accepting the changes you've made and starting to live your life differently

(4)

Based on the work of Adams, Hayes, Hopkins ..... TRANSITIONS published by Martin Robertson

MANAGING: WHAT'S DIFFERENT?

NEW & NOT ENJOYING IT?
THEN TRY .....

- Recognising what's happening (you're learning a new role;
  don't want to let yourself down; want to keep on good terms with staff)
- Seeking help from your boss or colleagues
- Doing something to establish yourself; even though you could well be
  unpopular
- Disciplining yourself; concentrate on priorities
- Learning to deal with difficult people,
  if they are the problem (see page 29 - 30 for some tips)
- Getting some training; remember there are ways to develop yourself
  other than courses (sometimes more effective) (see page 61)
- Being positive; try to focus on other aspects of the job, eg:
    - You are the person trusted with getting things done
    - You have power and influence over what's happening
    - You possess skills and abilities

Remember: *'The doors of opportunity are marked push'.*

(5)

STAFF KNOW MORE THAN YOU?
SIGNS

You find yourself managing staff with:
- more day to day knowledge of what's happening, or
- greater technical knowledge and skills

Typically:
- They use jargon that you don't know
- Give explanations that you don't understand and, what's more, cannot argue against
- You find yourself by-passed: people in the organisation go direct to others for an answer/explanation
- Feel yourself losing touch
- Try to keep yourself updated but things change so fast
- Have other demands on your time (eg: meetings, dealing with customers); your intentions are good but the situation is hopeless

STAFF KNOW MORE THAN YOU?
POSSIBLE REASONS

● The higher you move up the ladder into 'management' the further you could be getting away from the jobs that people do

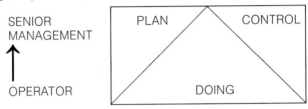

SENIOR MANAGEMENT

↑

OPERATOR

PLAN   CONTROL

DOING

● As an 'operator' you became an expert at your job

● In a managerial role you often lose that expertise and spend your time doing other things, such as planning and controlling the work of your section

● Sadly, often the higher you rise the less of an 'expert' you will become

(7)

STAFF KNOW MORE THAN YOU?
THEN TRY .....

- Recognising it; don't try to fight it
- Talking to people on a one-to-one basis to:
    - Identify and acknowledge their skills and clarify your skills and position
    - Explore how they can help you, eg: giving you information; getting known as the department expert
    - Explain how you can help them, e.g.:
        - By promoting them as individuals (giving them credit to a wider audience both inside and outside the organisation)
        - By making life more interesting for them
    - Ask them to keep you involved
- Asking for an explanation - especially if you're not sure what they are talking about and/or its implications
- Getting on and doing the job that you are paid for
- Seeking to educate people; experts can sometimes become rather narrow in their outlook

PEOPLE RESISTING CHANGE?
SIGNS

As a (new) manager you identify areas where changes need to be made. However, these are met by reactions that could include:

- Being given a list of reasons why ideas will not work, e.g.:
  - We've always done it this way; it works, so why change it?
- Shaking of heads - poor/no eye contact
- Quoting examples from the past: 'we've tried it before'

- Ganging up with others to resist new ways
- Saying 'yes' and doing nothing
- Always being too busy to listen to your new ideas
- Setting you up to fail!

PEOPLE RESISTING CHANGE?
POSSIBLE REASONS

- With you:
    - You're new to the job and want to make an impression
    - Seek to change things ..... possibly unnecessarily
    - May not have thought through the implications and how to sell change to others
- With them:
    - Personal dislike/distrust of you
    - Fear of the unknown / insecurity / fear of experimenting
    - Historical factors, relating to how previous situations have been handled
    - Misinformation; don't understand what's happening and why
    - People's core skills are threatened
    - Low trust within the organisation
    - Fear of failure, making mistakes, looking stupid
    - Strong peer group norms to conform to
    - Change comes from management; therefore oppose it

PEOPLE RESISTING CHANGE?

THEN TRY .....

- Planning - with any change think it through, e.g.:
    - Why are you changing? Is it your idea or something that's been imposed?
    - What are you trying to change - a method of working or the direction of your business?
    - What's going for it; what's going against it?
    - Who will be the winners/losers
    - What could go wrong?
    - How will you overcome any problems?
    - Who do you need to get on your side and by when?
    - Work out a timescale and the details of what has to be achieved
    - What support can you get from your boss or colleagues, especially if it's of major significance to the organisation?

Remember, where time allows there's no substitute for planning

PEOPLE RESISTING CHANGE?

THEN TRY .....

- Talking to them as individuals about the changes BUT don't be surprised if they behave differently when they are with their peers/in a group
- Involving them:
    - Discuss what needs to be done and get their ideas
    - Sell the benefits as you see them
    - Sow seeds to get them interested
    - Listen to any worries and concerns expressed; how can these be overcome?
    - Confront any potential problems at an early stage
- If they resist:
    - Agree a compromise: a trial period using a combination of their ideas and yours
    - Don't push it; you may be able to live without the change
    - Put it on ice: come back to it when the time/climate is more favourable

DEALING WITH PEOPLE

DEALING WITH PEOPLE

YOU CAN'T AVOID IT

- A large part of managing involves dealing with people, both inside and outside the organisation

- Often success depends on getting people to work (willingly) both for and with you. It sounds easy but problems occur with:
    - The difficult and unpredictable person
    - People you know but who surprise you by their (in)actions
    - Having to deal with people you don't necessarily like
    - Communication breakdowns: was it your fault or theirs?

- The key to dealing with people is the need to adapt the approach to individuals: what works for one may not necessarily work for another

- Insights as well as an understanding of people and personality may help you deal with some of the situations that follow

NO SUPPORT FROM BOSS?

SIGNS

On a variety of issues you feel that your boss is letting you down

- He or she is:
    - Not available when needed
    - Critical of your ideas
    - Always in a hurry ('Make it quick')

- He or she says:
  'If that's what you want to do, go ahead and I will back you; but then:
    - Doesn't
    - Criticises you afterwards
    - Holds it against you, often for years to come

- Is friendlier with the staff than with you

- Offers very little feedback; you don't know where you stand

- Gives you rope ..... and allows you to hang yourself

NO SUPPORT FROM BOSS?
POSSIBLE REASONS

- Boss believes that you are wrong; in his or her experience:
    - It will not work
    - You haven't thought through all the implications
- Boss is protecting himself/herself
- Is "two faced"
- Dislikes you
- Is not skilled at handling staff
- Does not trust your judgement, especially if you have made mistakes in the past
- Your boss has a demanding job and is often pre-occupied when you talk to him/her. Therefore he/she may not have grasped the total picture

- Politically, on the issues in question, boss gains very little from supporting you
- There has been a breakdown in communication between you

DEALING WITH PEOPLE

NO SUPPORT FROM BOSS?
THEN TRY .....

- Considering your options:
    - To do nothing would be to duck the issue
    - At the very least you have to find out why you are getting no support (you may learn something)
- Thinking back and asking yourself:
    - Am I sure that my boss doesn't support me? (Have you any facts or is it just a feeling/hunch?)
    - How important is it? Am I supported on the major issues and not on the minor ones (or vice versa)?
- What pressures is he/she under at present?
- Could you present your ideas more successfully? Tips include:
    - Thinking how your boss likes things presented
    - Asking what might be in it for him/her?
    - Anticipating objections he/she might raise?
    - Keeping your presentation simple
    - Being businesslike

(17)

DEALING WITH PEOPLE

NO SUPPORT FROM BOSS?
THEN TRY .....

Using the 3-part assertion message as a way of confronting your boss:
1. Prepare a non-judgemental description of his/her behaviour:
- Describe in **specific** rather than vague terms
- Limit yourself to **behavioural** descriptions; don't attempt to draw inferences
- Make it as brief as possible

2. Disclose your feelings:
- How do you feel about the effects of the other person's behaviour on you?

3. Say how this behaviour affects you

EXAMPLE:
Behaviour description	'When you disagreed with my decision on .....
Disclosure of feelings	I felt annoyed and let down .....
Effect on you	because I was counting on your support to make it happen.'

MOTIVATION DROPS?
SIGNS

Often you have a good member of staff who, for no apparent reason, appears to lose motivation. You might notice:

- Work output falls
- Lack of interest in job/organisation
- Person lets it be known that he/she is 'looking around for another job'
- Work is delayed; even the simplest job becomes a chore
- Arrives late ..... but leaves on time
- Clock watches ..... sighs a lot!
- His/her behaviour is rubbing off on others; all of a sudden many people seem disgruntled and unhappy

(19)

MOTIVATION DROPS?
POSSIBLE REASONS

- Motivation is a complex and personal topic:
    - What motivates one person, may not motivate another
    - It changes; individuals are motivated by particular things at certain times
- Consider what could be causing the situation. Is it:
    - The job, e.g.: no longer holds any challenge?
    - Job security or lack of it?
    - Money ..... not getting paid enough for the position and responsibilities?
    - Status ..... not being recognised?
    - Working conditions ..... sometimes have an effect on people's abilities to concentrate (e.g.: open plan offices are often difficult to work in)
    - Relationships with others?
    - Quality of supervision (or lack of it)?
    - Too much red tape making life difficult?
    - Something outside work?

MOTIVATION DROPS?
THEN TRY .....

- Considering how well you know the person:
  - Has it happened before?
  - When did you last talk to him/her about work or hobbies?
- Being clear about what you want the person to do differently/ better in the future
- Remembering that everybody (even the laziest person) is motivated to do **something;** the problem is that they are not motivated to do what you want them to do
- Making the individual aware of what he/she is (or is not) doing and the effect it's having. Remember, effective feedback concentrates on:
  - How people behave NOT the people themselves
  - What you've observed NOT what you've inferred
  - Sharing ideas NOT giving advice
  - Exploring alternatives NOT providing answers

MOTIVATION DROPS?

THEN TRY .....

- Not forgetting that motivation is a 2-way process: there are certain things you can do; the rest is down to the individual (you can take a horse to water but you can't make it drink)

- Considering what the person is good at and what he/she enjoys doing: then looking at the job; what chance is there for these skills and abilities to be used? Could you build in more opportunities?

- Building a challenge into the job:
    - Can you make it broader?
    - Are you able to delegate some of your work to the person ?
    - Can he/she take on more?

- Setting objectives or letting the person set his/her own as an aid to motivation (see page 98 for objective setting)

- Offering counselling especially if the problem is outside work and of a personal nature

DEALING WITH PEOPLE

A POOR PERFORMER?

SIGNS

You find yourself managing an individual whose work can only be described as 'poor'. Typically:

- The person never achieves ..... poor performance becomes the norm and consequently standards drop
- He/she cannot be relied on to deliver / misses deadlines
- Mistakes are made ..... he/she blames others and resents being spoken to
- You find yourself spending a lot of time with him/her
- When put under pressure the person panics
- It's having a knock-on effect:
    - Morale drops   - People start to complain
    - Others are having to pick up additional work which leads to resentment/bad atmosphere
- Difficulties are compounded, especially if the poor performer is managing/supervising others!

A POOR PERFORMER?
POSSIBLE REASONS

- Person has reached the limit of capability
- Is not aware that performance is poor
- Has never been confronted/told before
- It could be:
  - You: e.g.: standards are too high for the individual
  - The Work: e.g.: too difficult, too much, person becomes demotivated
  - The Individual: e.g.: unhappy, in poor health, lazy
- Apathy amongst management
  - People are aware of the problem/situation but nobody has been prepared to do anything about it

DEALING WITH PEOPLE

A POOR PERFORMER?
THEN TRY .....

- Getting to the core of the problem:
    - Don't simply address the symptoms
- Remembering that:
    - As a manager you are responsible for the performance of your staff
    - Your credibility could be on the line if you don't do anything about it
      (irrespective of what's happened in the past)
    - Covering up for the individual will be evading the issue
    - If someone claims to have a certain skill they must be able to
      demonstrate it
    - You can dismiss someone for poor performance if they are:
        - Incapable of performing
        - Capable but their work falls below the required standard
      Ask yourself if the person falls into either of these categories? If 'yes',
      start to put in place any company procedures for dealing with these
      situations

A POOR PERFORMER?

THEN TRY .....

- Going back to basics, e.g.:
    - What do you expect the person to do?
    - How well/to what standard should he or she perform?
    - Identify where people may be falling down; be specific and try to establish why this is
    - Obtain agreement on:
        - What needs to be done
        - What help is needed
        - A timescale
    - Put the points in writing (this is essential especially if your plan fails to bring about an improvement in performance)
    - Give any support that you agreed to provide
    - Monitor the person's performance and take any action that may be necessary, as you go along

'DIFFICULT' INDIVIDUAL?

SIGNS

Have you come across an individual who performs well but whose behaviour can only be described as 'difficult'? Someone who:

- Disagrees a lot
- Is unco-operative
- Often avoids eye contact
- Is unpredictable (blows hot and cold) or moody
- Gets angry/annoyed with you and others
- Sometimes acts the 'loner' (may not mix with the rest of the group/team)
- Says 'yes' and does nothing
- Does the minimum required and often little more
- Behaves badly to other people, e.g.:
    - Attempts to put people down (in front of others)
    - Makes sexist/racist remarks
    - Goes behind people's backs

(27)

DEALING WITH PEOPLE

'DIFFICULT' INDIVIDUAL?
POSSIBLE REASONS

- Holds a grudge
- Lonely or shy
- Troubled by something outside work
- Dislikes the job
- Resents you or your seniority
- Dislikes being supervised
- Feels badly done by
- Frustrated
- Feels anxious and nervous which
  can affect behaviour
- May face conflict over values, beliefs or personality
- Could be working on the wrong/different assumptions
- Wants to draw attention to himself/herself
- Is playing a game

DEALING WITH PEOPLE

'DIFFICULT' INDIVIDUAL?

THEN TRY .....

- Accepting that it may not be the person who is difficult but his or her behaviour
- Thinking about the 'difficult' person:
    - In what situation is he/she difficult?
    - What is it about his or her behaviour that's 'difficult'?
    - How do you behave when he or she is 'difficult'?
    - What triggers that behaviour off in him/her?
    - What happens afterwards in both of you? Is there a pattern emerging?
- Identifying the behaviour that you find 'difficult': can you put a label on it? (If so this will help you deal with it)
- Recognising how you feel when it happens, e.g.: overwhelmed/helpless; in control; aggressive/worked up
- Both believing and behaving in a way that demonstrates that you are in control of your own thoughts and subsequent actions

'DIFFICULT' INDIVIDUAL?
THEN TRY .....

- Considering your options, e.g.:
  - Do nothing especially if you suspect that you know the underlying reason for the behaviour
  - Learn to live with it   - Stand up to him or her
  - Go for a compromise   - Play for time
  - Behave in the same way towards the person
  - Use the power of your position to put him/her down
  - Ask for help to be able to deal with him/her
- Developing skills to deal with people/situations, e.g.:-
  - Learning to be assertive as a means of:
    - Controlling your emotions
    - Telling people how they are behaving, how you feel and what you want them to do/not do in the future
  - Improving your listening ability
  - Improving your confrontational styles

PERSISTENT LATECOMER?

SIGNS

How do you manage a person who is often absent at the start of the day? Someone who:

- Creeps in after the official starting time and hopes not to be noticed
- Always .....
    - makes excuses when confronted (often with a twinkle in the eye)
    - promises to improve ..... and does so for two days before slipping back into old habits

- Arrives late for meetings and often fails to meet deadlines

- Despite coming in late, stays to make up time at the end of the day ..... 'I make up my hours ..... so what's the problem?'

PERSISTENT LATECOMER?
POSSIBLE REASONS

- May have genuine reasons for being late, e.g.:
    - has to make domestic arrangements for children or elderly relatives
    - has a difficult journey to work
      that relies upon public transport

- Unable to get up in the mornings .....
  for a variety of reasons .....
  burning the candle at both ends?

- Disorganised or a disaster-prone individual whose life is in a mess

- The individual does not consider it a serious issue ('no big deal') and does

  not make the effort

DEALING WITH PEOPLE

PERSISTENT LATECOMER?

THEN TRY

- Identifying the problem you are having personally with the lateness. Is it .....
    - the fact that the person arrives late?
    - that others have to cover up/make excuses?
    - the disruption caused by the late arrival?
    - that your authority as manager is being undermined?
- Working out a strategy for dealing with the person
    - you could do nothing, as it may not be serious, merely irritating - BUT .....
        - others may notice and pass comment
        - standards may fall
        - punctual people may feel resentful
        - absence at key times causes problems
    - keep a diary and get the **facts:** is there a trend emerging?
    - if it's irritating, caution the person but point out that you may be forced to take action if things don't improve
    - if it's serious, then take advice - there may be procedures within your organisation that you should/could follow

DEALING WITH PEOPLE

PERSISTENT LATECOMER?
THEN TRY

- Confronting the individual
    - explain what has happened and feedback any observations you've made
    - ask for an explanation
    Tip ..... do this on a one-to-one basis, preferably in your office or away from the workgroup.
- Checking that he or she is aware of any rules regarding timekeeping
- Explaining:
    - what you want and why (stress the impact of poor time keeping on others)
    - what you propose to do about the lateness and why
    - what help, if any, you can offer
    - how you will monitor the situation

With the person who doesn't regard it as a serious issue you have to:
    - tell the person how you feel (you do regard it as a serious issue)
    - reach some form of understanding, e.g. agreeing to accept the situation, re-scheduling hours or informing him/her that you will not let the issue drop

BOSS DECIDES WITHOUT YOU?

SIGNS

There may be occasions when your boss makes a decision which directly affects you or your department without consulting you.

- You're often not told about it; worse still you find out from others ..... your staff
- Not consulted; meetings happen to which you're not invited
- You hear a rumour and:
  - Ignore it; it can't be true or
  - You confront your boss only to be told:
    1. 'It doesn't affect you'
    2. 'There's nothing to worry about'

OR

- You are consulted and asked for your views, but:
  - These are ignored
  - It's a token gesture; the plans are in place despite you

BOSS DECIDES WITHOUT YOU?
POSSIBLE REASONS

It could be that the boss:
- Is playing organisational politics:
    - It's part of something bigger happening in the organisation
    - He or she knows something that you don't
- Is under pressure:
    - There's not enough time to consult; possibly you weren't available
- Feels that you lack experience
- Doesn't value your opinion, ideas and experience
- Could be trying to tell you something
- Wants to exert himself/ herself ('macho management')
- Is under-occupied so interferes in your domain

(Don't forget that as a manager you very often have to 'sell' the decisions of those above you to your staff)

DEALING WITH PEOPLE

BOSS DECIDES WITHOUT YOU?
THEN TRY .....

- Doing nothing on the basis that:
    - It may be a one off
    - You can live with it
    - Is it **really** that important?

    Note: The dangers of this approach are:
    - You could take it upon yourself to worry (this can cause you much anxiety and stress)
    - You could be perceived as being weak:
        1. By the boss (who may have set you up)
        2. By your staff (for not standing up to your boss)
    - It could happen again, then what would you do?

- Saying something; after all you have a choice ranging from:

| Avoiding the situation | ← | Defusing the situation | → | Confronting the situation |

BOSS DECIDES WITHOUT YOU?
THEN TRY .....

- Confronting your boss; two possible ways are:
    - Straight 'power play' (you are using your power/your boss is using his/hers); beware, with this approach you may not win!
    - Negotiating by being assertive: acting within your own rights at the same time respecting the needs and feelings of others; examples of language to use:

SELF-DISCLOSURE	'My situation is .....'
	'That makes me feel .....'
DEMANDING	'I want, think, feel, need .....'
PERSISTING	'I appreciate your point, but I need .....'

Tip If you are expected to sell the decision to your staff then:
- Firstly, clear any concerns you have with your boss
- Find out the reasons and thinking behind the decision
- Jointly discuss potential problems and how they can be overcome
- If possible get your boss to be there with you

DEALING WITH PEOPLE

OPPOSING VIEWS ON STAFF?
SIGNS

Sometimes you and your boss hold conflicting opinions on the abilities of people/staff reporting to you:

- Boss tells you so
- Looks to 'promote' others who you do not rate so highly
- Tends to dismiss your views of people
- Sees things in others that you don't
- Focuses on someone's good points ..... ignores the bad
- Looks for opportunities to prove a point about his/her chosen candidate ..... 'there, I told you so .....'

OPPOSING VIEWS ON STAFF?
POSSIBLE REASONS

- Boss is a better judge of people than you
    - More experienced
    - More skilled at spotting potential
- Could be testing you:
    - To see how good your judgement is, or
    - Is the argumentative type
- Different standards:
    - Boss's interpretation of 'good' is different from yours
- Boss may be impressionable:
    - Forms opinions (good/bad) based on one or two events,
      or even on first impressions
- Might know something that you don't
- You could be blinkered in your approach/views of people:
    - Want to promote or protect them
    - Always see good/bad side of a person
    - You too could be forming your views based on one or two events

DEALING WITH PEOPLE

OPPOSING VIEWS ON STAFF?

THEN TRY .....

- Listening to your boss:
  - What are his or her reasons, and why?   - Based on what evidence?
- Presenting your case:
  - Do so positively   - Work on **facts** not emotions
- Not being afraid to challenge, but do so constructively
- If you want to present a different view:
  - Listen to what the person is saying - Repeat it back in your own words
  - Use a linking word, such as .....

    However'   'On the other hand'
    'Nevertheless'   'Alternatively'
    ..... before you present your view
- Keep an open mind:
  - Is there something you missed in your assessment?
  - What could you learn by listening to your boss?

CLASH OVER APPRAISAL?
SIGNS

Very often an individual disagrees with your assessment of him or her at appraisal time and either:

- Tells you direct, or

- Does not say so directly but makes sure you:
    - Overhear his/her views as you are passing by
    - Hear him/her running the appraisal down, for a variety of reasons, to work colleagues
    - Hear via a third party

CLASH OVER APPRAISAL?
POSSIBLE REASONS

- Personality clash

- Individual genuinely believes that he/she is better than your assessment

- Appraisal system is limited, i.e.:
    - May be one way (you appraising them)
    - A 'tick in the box' style which limits choice and discussion

- As the boss you have contributed to the situation by:
    - saving any complaints until the appraisal time
    - not confronting any situations (i.e. regarding performance) earlier
    - not explaining clearly to the individual the appraisal system,
      its purpose and methods
    - being poorly trained (if at all) in conducting appraisals

CLASH OVER APPRAISAL?

THEN TRY .....

- Making sure you know your organisation's appraisal system; if in doubt ask
- Not avoiding the situation (any dissatisfaction could have a longer-term effect)
- Talking to the individual:
  - 'Exactly what do you disagree with and why?'
  - 'What do you think it should be and why?'
- Being clear in your own mind what you think of the individual and why; remember, if you are commenting on performance get the **facts.** Be specific.
- Agreeing on any common ground
- Identifying the sticking point
- Attempting to compromise and reach a 'win-win' situation
- Offering a way out if the person is still not satisfied (e.g.: an appeal to a third party)

FINALLY: When it's all over and settled, use it as a learning experience, e.g.: how could the situation have been avoided and what would you do differently next time?

HEAVY DRINKER?

SIGNS

You are concerned about an individual who often:
- Arrives late
- Smells of drink (possibly a hangover)
- Has an unkempt physical appearance and puts on/loses weight, etc
- Is frequently absent (e.g.: stomach upsets)
- Is unpredictable (moody, very high/low)
- Speaks in a slurred manner
- Disappears for long periods
- In a world of his/her own
- May borrow money; always broke
- Is recognisably 'drunk' at work
- Gets drunk at office parties and 'occasions'
- Is known by others to have a 'problem' but people are too embarrassed to say anything

(45)

DEALING WITH PEOPLE

HEAVY DRINKER?
POSSIBLE REASONS

- Individual is going through a difficult time (e.g.: bereavement, illness, depression, break up of a relationship)
- Lives away from home
- Easily led; in with a bad crowd

NOTE

If somebody has a 'problem' it may lead - albeit temporarily - to drink. Should the 'problem' improve or sort itself out then very often the drinking problem will subside.

However, somebody who makes a habit of drinking too much alcohol could have a more serious problem, that of being an alcoholic.

Alcoholics don't need a reason and will always justify their drinking with more reasons and excuses than space permits us to list here!

HEAVY DRINKER?

THEN TRY .....

- Bearing in mind that:

    - People may never drink at work, yet their work may suffer as a consequence of alcoholism

    - Somebody who happens to drink at work is not necessarily an alcoholic

- Using counselling rather than disciplining to help somebody who is dependent on alcohol

    - Employees suffering from alcoholism should not be dismissed if they are willing to accept treatment

- Asking yourself the $64,000 question: 'is it a drink problem or alcoholism?'

DEALING WITH PEOPLE

HEAVY DRINKER?
THEN TRY .....

- Observing the person over a period of time:
    - If you know there is a 'life problem' deal with it via counselling and support
    - Generally speaking, such a person will only be too willing to try anything to feel better and be quite happy to quit drinking
    - Should this not be successful and the behaviour continues, then you could be dealing with an alcoholic
- If it's alcoholism, then try:
    - Encouraging the individual to identify it
    - Getting **them** to contact AA or suggesting that they contact their own doctor with the support of a friend, colleague or family if necessary
    - Bearing in mind that you will have only limited or often no success in helping alcoholics who have not recognised or admitted their problem; often they will keep reverting to the 'reasons' and carry on drinking ('After all you would drink if you have my problems ..... it's what helps me to cope')

Thanks to JRH

PERSON HAS B.O.?

SIGNS

There's something unpleasant about a person that makes you
not want to spend too long in their company. You notice that:

- Individual is avoided and possibly
  isolated by others
- Called nicknames
- Gets a reputation: nobody wants
  to be left in the same room as the person
- People play games: send bars of soap,
  put deodorants in the drawer/locker
- There's gossip behind the person's back
- You are aware of the problem but have resisted
  saying anything as you hope that it will go away
- Everybody knows but nobody has told the individual

PERSON HAS B.O.?
POSSIBLE REASONS

- Person is lazy, doesn't bother to wash

- Doesn't change clothes

- Could be a medical problem (e.g.: anxiety can lead to over active glands)

- A domestic problem: the person may have left home and is living/sleeping rough

- Person may be unaware that there's a problem

DEALING WITH PEOPLE

PERSON HAS B.O.?
THEN TRY ....

- Confronting the individual by using the **SNAP** technique:

S pecify the situation: 'It's been drawn to my attention that you have a problem of a personal nature regarding body odour'

N ame your feelings: 'I am concerned that this might cause you some embarrassment'

A sk: 'I would ask you to pay greater attention to this aspect of personal hygiene'

P ayoff
POSITIVE: 'This will help you overcome a difficult situation'
NEGATIVE: 'Otherwise I fear you run the risk of being isolated by your colleagues'

(For a fuller explanation of the **SNAP** technique see 'The Interviewer's Pocketbook' by John Townsend published by Management Pocketbooks)

What if nothing happens? Seek advice from the Human Resources and/or Medical Departments as well as anybody who may know the individual

DEVELOPING ABILITIES

DEVELOPING ABILITIES

WHY IT'S IMPORTANT

The need to train and develop people is key to ensuring success in today's competitive market. Consider that:
- People are a valuable resource - second only to customers?
- All the 'profits' of the organisation are generated by the efforts of people
- Everybody has ability; most people are simply looking for a chance to use it
- Business and personal needs are constantly changing - training is an investment for the future which helps to maintain and improve your organisation's position in the marketplace
- Your reputation as an employer will be enhanced as will your ability to attract high calibre staff
- It could save you money and may well be cheaper in the long run

Remember
   When planning for a year - sow corn
   When planning for a decade - plant trees
   When planning for a lifetime - train and educate people

DEVELOPING ABILITIES

DIFFICULTY SETTLING IN?

SIGNS

You take on staff who, each in their own way, have problems settling in and may be showing signs of stress. For example:

- 16-year-old **school leaver** who:
  - rarely says a word, blushes easily and doesn't know what to call people
- **20-year-old** with work experience who despite being bright at the interview:
  - gives the impression of not enjoying the job, of being bored and moody
  - is not showing the promise that you had hoped
- Experienced person, who has been doing a **similar job** in another organisation, who is:
  - not coping with the workload and is always comparing your organisation with their previous one
  - being seen as a 'know-it-all' by others
- An individual **returning to work** after a period of absence who appears to be:
  - struggling with the technology and systems
  - having difficulty relating to a younger supervisor/work colleagues

DEVELOPING ABILITIES

DIFFICULTY SETTLING IN?
POSSIBLE REASONS

- **School leaver:** for whom it's a whole new experience, i.e.
    - Is working longer hours - has new skills to pick up
    - Coming into contact with different (often older) people
- **20-year old:**
    - Could be having problems learning a new job
    - Has less experience than you assumed
    - Is working to different routines, standards, style of management
- Person doing a **similar job:**
    - Could be having difficulty fitting in ..... possibly at a higher/lower level
    - May have spent a long time (whole career?) in last company and is having problems adjusting to the change
- **Returner:**
    - Having to adjust to a different routine (e.g.: previously managed own time ..... now it's dictated by others)
    - Has to balance work and non-work activities
    - Much has changed during the period that he or she was away

DEVELOPING ABILITIES

DIFFICULTY SETTLING IN?
THEN TRY .....

- **School leaver:**
  - Making person feel welcome   - Putting him/her with someone of own age group   - Giving feedback and praise at an early stage
  - Using others for support

Remember, don't assume that the person is confident; it could be a false image

- **20-year old:**
  - Recognising potential problems (e.g.: coming from a totally different job/industry)
  - Providing help during the early stages
  - Not assuming that because person has been working before, that he/she will find it easy to fit in
  - Asking them to give you a weekly report on
    - what they have been doing
    - how they have been getting on, anything they've found difficult
    - any possible ways that things could be done differently (don't forget the benefit of a fresh pair of eyes)

DEVELOPING ABILITIES

DIFFICULTY SETTLING IN?

THEN TRY .....

- Person doing a **similar job:**
  - Finding out **exactly** what individual did in last job and .....
  - Identifying any differences in systems/procedures (can **you** learn from previous methods?)
  - Setting standards and ensuring that they can be met (give help if necessary)
  - Watching for signs that the person is getting on with colleagues
- **Returner:**
  - Talking about potential difficulties at the time of the interview and ideas for overcoming them
  - Possibly introducing the person gradually to work (e.g.: build up their hours)
  - Arranging a comprehensive induction programme to include - if necessary - new technology
  - Making person feel wanted by asking for ideas (remember everybody has something to offer)

CAN'T AFFORD COURSES?
SIGNS

Things are happening that indicate that staff would benefit from training

- Poor/low standard of performance
- Lack of motivation
- Complaints from customers and staff
- Frequent mistakes
- Long time taken to do tasks
- Requests for help and assistance
- It is the intention to introduce a new system or method of working

You make suggestions and requests for courses but nothing happens:
'too expensive' is the answer you get back.

DEVELOPING ABILITIES

CAN'T AFFORD COURSES?
POSSIBLE REASONS

- Money is tight:
    - You have not estimated for it
    - Spent what money you have
- Historical:
    - No evidence that training has worked in the past
- It's a fine balancing act between:
    - Getting the job done, albeit with difficulties, and .....
    - ..... investing time now to reap long-term benefits
- You are busy (e.g.: through seasonal demands) and can't afford staff away from work
- Lack of staff:
    - Absence (illness or holidays)
    - Left and can't be replaced (we're cutting back on staff)
- Your limited view of training (e.g.: training = courses)

DEVELOPING ABILITIES

CAN'T AFFORD COURSES?
THEN TRY .....

- Remembering that not all problems or needs can be 'solved' by training (e.g.: lack of motivation may require actions other than sending a person on a course. See pages 21-2)
- Being aware that courses have limited success unless the individual is encouraged to use in his/her job the skills and knowledge learnt.
- Recognising that there are many ways of helping people learn (each with its pros and cons) other than courses e.g.:
  - Watching people • Standing in • Meetings • Task forces • Visiting other departments/companies • From each other • One-to-one sessions • Reading • Watching a video • Making mistakes • Discussions • Role plays • Being thrown in at deep end • Manuals • Talking to an expert
- Using learning opportunities which occur at the work place; many are quicker and more cost-effective than sending people on courses
- Making a positive commitment to look for and use such internal training
  - **it will not happen by itself**

DEVELOPING ABILITIES

CAN'T AFFORD COURSES?
THEN TRY .....

- Recognising the role you can play as a trainer at work (e.g. influencing performance via personal example, demonstration, setting standards)
- Adding coaching to your list of skills:
  - this involves HELPING people find solutions to current work problems, but in such a way that they LEARN whilst doing this
  - the purpose is to develop them to reach their full potential and/or help them overcome current difficulties
- Using day to day work as a learning opportunity by
  - looking for coaching opportunities
  - being prepared to take risks of delegating important tasks
  - identifying coaching tasks which stretch individuals
  - coaching staff who are succeeding, as well as those requiring help
  - unearthing ideas by questioning and listening . . . . offering guidance rather than solutions and . . . . not finding fault or attaching blame if people make mistakes when being coached.

(Source: Roger Acland)

BOSS AGAINST TRAINING?
SIGNS

How do you deal with a boss who doesn't believe in training? Someone who:
- Makes statements like:
  'You don't learn from courses, you learn from experience'
  (This could be true ..... but how do we know that we learn from the same experience?)
  'Not been on a course for years ..... I've managed to avoid them'
  'We spend the money ..... person leaves ..... and others get the benefit. What sense does that make?'
- If you've been on a learning event, boss doesn't:
    - Ask you how you got on, or
    - Encourage you to try new ways, or
    - Encourage you to pass on your knowledge to others
- Does not tell you when training events become available; you find out from others
- Replies to any requests for training by saying 'leave it to me' but nothing happens

BOSS AGAINST TRAINING?

POSSIBLE REASONS

Could genuinely resist training due to:
- Poor personal experiences of training
- Historical:
    - His/her boss never showed encouragement
    - Poor personal example from others
- Fear of:
    - Being shown up/exposed   - Others doing a better job
    - Staff improving their skills, confidence and abilities, enabling them to move on and progress
- Poor image of training
    - The way it's sold and presented   - It's seen simply as courses with little relevance to business or individual needs
    - Training department lacks credibility within the company
- Organisational:
    - Training has to be paid for out of departmental budget and there may be other priorities

BOSS AGAINST TRAINING?

THEN TRY .....

- Identifying the form of resistance: (see ideas on resisting change page 12)
    - What arguments does your boss use and why?
    - How could you counter them?
- Working out a strategy for persuasion:
    - What do you want to achieve?
    - What's involved ..... step by step?
    - How will you present your case?
      (see page 17 for ideas)
    - When is the best time to broach the
      subject - is your boss a 'morning' or
      'afternoon' person?
    - What happens if the answer is 'No'?
    - What's your fallback position should
      this happen?

DEVELOPING ABILITIES

BOSS AGAINST TRAINING?
THEN TRY .....

- Preparing and making your case:
    - What training do you want and why?
    - Where is it to be held and what's involved?
      (Remember there are ways of training other than holding courses;
      see page 61)
    - What improvements can be expected? Show how the money spent will
      benefit .....
        - You
        - The organisation
        - Your department
        - Him or her as a boss
      ..... through improved job performance and productivity
- Giving examples of how it helped other individuals and departments
- Enlisting support from:
    - Others in your group
    - People who have attended similar training
    - A credible training department

DEVELOPING ABILITIES

A SLOW LEARNER?
SIGNS

One of your staff takes a while to pick things up:

- Despite devoting a lot of time, energy and effort to the person there's still no visible sign of improvement

- The individual is a careful worker and often methodically checks own work

- Works at one pace

- Possibly keeps making mistakes

- Rejects offers of assistance: 'I'm okay ..... I don't need any help, thanks'

- The result is that you often get exasperated, and find yourself explaining things over and over again

DEVELOPING ABILITIES

A SLOW LEARNER?
POSSIBLE REASONS

- Historical: didn't like or do well at school, consequently learning may be a difficult process
- Lack of confidence
- Shown up by others
- Trying too hard
- The training approach is wrong, e.g.:
    - Not geared to the level of the individual
    - Hasn't identified what might be blocking their learning process; it could be:
        - Perceptual (not seeing there's a problem)
        - Cultural (organisation does not support learning)
        - Emotional (fear of insecurity/mistakes)
        - Motivational (unwilling to take risks)
        - Environmental (place/time that training takes place)
        - Not geared to individual's preferred learning style

A SLOW LEARNER?

THEN TRY .....

Working through the following
- Identifying what needs to be learnt

- Assessing previous experience: what does
the person know and what is he/she capable of?
If in doubt check it out, i.e. 'test' the person, ask
for an explanation or demonstration of skills

- Assessing the difference between the two:
what is known and what can be done, as opposed
to what's required; any gap will identify what needs
to be learnt

- Breaking learning into manageable parts

- Identifying barriers to learning: **check them out** with the individual

(69)

DEVELOPING ABILITIES

A SLOW LEARNER?
THEN TRY .....

- Drawing up a learning plan:
    - What needs to be learnt and by when?
    - To what standard?
    - Potential barriers?
    - Preferred style of learning?
  Again check this out with the individual so that he/she knows what to expect

- Delivering the training; points to bear in mind include:
    - Check, as you go along, their understanding of any terms/jargon used
    - Where possible, encourage the individual to ask questions, preferably before giving instructions
    - Allow plenty of time for practice
    - If possible, encourage learning by mistakes (what went wrong and how could this have been avoided?)
    - Give any feedback in an objective way, highlighting both positive and negative aspects of performance

APPRAISALS NOT WORKING?

SIGNS

As part of a wider performance management system there exists a formal appraisal scheme or Personal Development Review. Unfortunately this often meets with a cynical response. It's not untypical that:

- There's little enthusiasm from staff and often - in truth - from you!
- You overhear comments such as:
  'Here we go again'
  'Annual ritual'
  'Personnel justifying their existence'
- If forms are used, they are often filled in poorly
- People avoid the date for the meeting
- Appraisal discussion is difficult:
  - Both parties feel awkward
  - Comments are made that reveal cynicism, from both sides
  - On the face of it, you would rather be doing other, more productive tasks
- Very little comes from them

APPRAISALS NOT WORKING?
POSSIBLE REASONS

- Historical factors:
    - Nothing has happened in the past as a result of appraisals
- Ignorance:
    - About the scheme; what it's meant to do
    - How it helps the organisation and the individual
    - Where it fits in to the performance management system
- Appraisal forms don't complement the performance management system
- Appraisal system is trying to do too much, i.e. review previous objectives and set new ones, identify staff with potential, collect training needs on a company-wide basis
- Staff aren't trained in the system and how to conduct formal appraisals
- Concept of appraisals often raises emotive issues; the system could be linked to:
    - Grading people (e.g.: A → E, reflecting excellent to poor) or, worse still ..... to pay awards

APPRAISALS NOT WORKING?

THEN TRY .....

- Remembering that appraisals - as a way of helping develop people's abilities - can be used to talk about current performance, agree future objectives and identify areas of help required

    - Formal appraisals are an attempt to force the appraiser and appraisee to have a discussion once a year

    - However, informal appraisals take place every working day, i.e. you witness somebody performing a task and form a conclusion

    - If, at the time, you are unhappy with what you see, then the individual needs to be told. Don't wait till appraisal time to store up all the grievances of the past twelve months

    - Don't blame any appraisal system for something that you should be doing on a regular basis - namely appraising, assessing staff; giving them feedback as well as the skills and confidence to perform

(73)

74

BUILDING TEAMS

BUILDING TEAMS

WHY IT'S IMPORTANT

Having got your collection of trained individuals you now have the opportunity to build them into a team.

'A team is a collection of individuals assembled for a specific purpose'

Team building can help:
- Tackle problems and opportunities faced
- Achieve commitment to the task/job in hand
- Encourage flexibility in a changing environment
- Allow individuals to grow in skills and confidence
- Develop openness and trust amongst members

On the downside
- Team-building can be time consuming
- Individuals may lose their identity
- 'The team' could become the vehicle for criticism by others in the organisation
- Teams may not always produce better decisions than those made by experts

PEOPLE NOT INTERESTED?
SIGNS

You start to try to build your team but find a lack of interest

- All attempts to get them to work, think and act as a team are ignored

- People continue to work as individuals, behaving in ways that conflict with all
  you are trying to promote, such as:
    - Not consulting their colleagues
    - Not considering other people's views
    - Working to their own objectives,
      regardless of the effect upon others

- When you get them together:
    - Energy is low
    - Ideas are few
    - Yours is the only voice heard
    - Their non verbals say it all!

PEOPLE NOT INTERESTED?
POSSIBLE REASONS

- Maybe there is no need to form a team; the nature of the work and type of organisation may preclude or make teamwork difficult:

  - Geographical divisions

  - People are used to working independently

  - Wage structure encourages/rewards personal performance, therefore people tend to look after themselves

- There could be conflict within the group which has not been resolved

- Yet again, historical: 'We've tried that before'

- Benefits of team-building/working are either poorly sold or not understood: each person has own idea/concept of a team

(78)

PEOPLE NOT INTERESTED?

THEN TRY .....

Considering whether you need to be a team? There's a difference between:

A co-operative group　　　and　　**An effective team**

- People work together
- Feelings aren't part of work
- Conflict is accommodated
- Trust and openness are measured
- Information passed on a 'need-to-know' basis
- Goals/objectives are either personal or unclear

- People trust each other
- Feelings expressed openly
- Conflict is worked through
- People support each other
- Information shared freely
- Objectives common to all

Remember, you need a team when:

- There's uncertainty about the job and the task in hand
- The task requires openness, shared ideas/feelings and trust
- There are genuine problems to face and ..... people are prepared to have a go at tackling them

(79)

BUILDING TEAMS

PEOPLE NOT INTERESTED?
THEN TRY .....

If you need and want to be a team, try to:
- Look for opportunities to build teamworking into your daily activities, i.e. get people working together on projects, thereby sharing ideas and skills
- Look for examples where teamworking has paid off, i.e. in sport, within your organisation. What can you learn from them?
- Share information and involve your people - if you don't, it's not surprising if they are not interested
- Hand over tasks to your people, ask for suggestions as to how it could be done. If it makes sense, let them do it
- Publish and have visible your goals and objectives (remember: the first two letters of 'goal' spell GO)
- Put together some teambuilding activities - there's plenty of material around should you want to run your own sessions
- Avoid getting carried away with WHAT you are doing but examine HOW you are doing things. What could you do differently?
- Encourage harmony - watch for 'them and us' situations

LEADERSHIP STYLE RESENTED?

SIGNS

There are a variety of ways in which you can lead a team. It could be that not everybody is happy with the style that you display:

- Staff tell you:
  - Directly and to your face
  - Indirectly (switch off when you approach them)
- You are compared with others ..... Hitler
- You get a nickname and a reputation
- It gets personal
- Team-building becomes difficult
- You get frustrated at:
  - Staff reactions
  - Your inability to make things happen

LEADERSHIP STYLE RESENTED?
POSSIBLE REASONS

- Perhaps you got it wrong?
  - Came in heavy or clumsy when there was no need
  - Panicked/over-reacted to situations
  - Were insensitive
  - The group set you up

- Perhaps it is the group?
  - Not used to your style; last leader was different
  - It's a reaction to change
  - Strong personalities within the group who would resent anybody!

- It could be that you've used the wrong style at the wrong time (see page 83)

LEADERSHIP STYLE RESENTED?

THEN TRY .....

- Acknowledging that there's a problem, i.e. if your leadership style is causing difficulty, then something has to change. Remember .....**Things don't change, we change**
  Should you adopt the attitude of 'take it or leave it' (and there are a lot of people who do) then don't be surprised if the number of takers is small

- Remembering that leadership is about influencing people's behaviour to achieve goals. A good leader is able to select a style to suit the circumstances
  No matter how many styles you have in your armoury from:
    - Directing and telling people (which has limited impact after a period of time)
    - Consulting (involving others in decision-making)
    - Collaborating (jointly agreeing what needs to be done)
    - Delegating (giving people tasks to do with the appropriate authority)
  they are of limited use if you fail to inspire people and lead by personal example

(83)

LEADERSHIP STYLE RESENTED?

THEN TRY .....

- **Inspiring** people with the will to win and be better than the opposition/competition. Ideas include:
    - being visible (MBWA ..... Managing by Walking About)
    - getting close to the action (don't hide in (head) office)
    - talking to customers as well as end users of your products/services
    - speaking to those who do the job to get their views, ideas, opinions, frustrations and suggestions
    - supporting people in difficult times
- **Leading by personal example** and from the front, as you'll be judged by what you do not by what you say
    - getting people involved - without this you'll get no commitment
    - being open minded, encouraging and showing confidence in any new ideas and suggestions (more *what if's* ..... fewer *yes but's*)
    - demonstrating energy ..... if you don't how can you expect it from them?
    - being true to your people. NEVER run them down in front of others ..... look to support and promote them in public

INDIVIDUAL IS ISOLATED?
SIGNS

Despite efforts to get people working together you notice that one person is being left out. Typically that individual:

- Doesn't join in
- Sits alone at break and meal times
- Appears tohave few friends
- Makes little contribution to meetings or discussions
- The group makes remarks about the individual
    - Sets the person up, or possibly .....
    - ..... picks on him/her
    - People snigger when his/her name is mentioned

INDIVIDUAL IS ISOLATED?
POSSIBLE REASONS

- That's how the individual wants it to be

- Shyness; mixing is difficult

- Individual dislikes work colleagues; suffers them but does not share their interests, values and ideas

- Historical; one person in the group holds a vendetta against the individual for whatever reason

- Individual may have a problem of a personal nature, e.g.: B.O.

- Individual is not very good at job and colleagues resent this

BUILDING TEAMS

INDIVIDUAL IS ISOLATED?
THEN TRY .....

- Watching exactly what happens and how often
    - Does it matter? It could if it's:
        - Making team-building difficult
        - Getting personal and vindictive
- Talking to the individual, e.g.:
  'I've noticed that you don't appear to mix with the others - is anything wrong?..... Why is this?'
  Follow up with further probing questions to seek specific information
- Finding out why they are behaving this way, i.e. is it a feeling that they have nothing/very little to give?
- Considering the implications of their behaviour on the team. Remember there's often little you can do to force the person to join in. However, depending on the amount of damage that's being caused, you may have to confront them or even remove them from the team

BUILDING TEAMS

INDIVIDUAL IS ISOLATED?
THEN TRY .....

- Giving them an opportunity to succeed (especially if you believe that they have something to offer) by:

    - providing them with a chance to contribute, i.e. bring them into meetings, ask for ideas
    - setting up teams which deliberately involve them in sharing their knowledge, skills and experiences with others
    - getting them to head up a project, task or exercise
    - giving them feedback and encouragement

- Running a team building event that brings out the issues of participation, involvement and commitment. Then turn it back to your own team, i.e. 'How would we measure ourselves .....?'

LEADERSHIP CHALLENGED?
SIGNS

For no apparent reason one of your group fancies themselves as the leader

- You become aware that an individual:

  - Is acting as if he or she is in charge, e.g.: giving orders, making decisions

  - Challenges you, both one-to-one and at meetings

  - Enlists support against you from:
    1 Work group, or even .....
    2 ..... other managers

OR

- You are not aware of it and fail to read any of the above signs

LEADERSHIP CHALLENGED?
POSSIBLE REASONS

- Individual believes himself/herself to be better than you

- Jealousy: you have the job that he/she wanted

- Is doing it to test you

- Insecurity

- As a way of drawing attention to himself/herself

- Put up to it by somebody else for whatever reason

BUILDING TEAMS

LEADERSHIP CHALLENGED?
THEN TRY .....

- Confronting person head on by re-asserting your role as leader (use this when you want to put a quick end to the situation)

- Developing your own skills of persuasion:
    - Can you get individual on your side, working with and not against you?
    - Be more assertive and firmer

- Doing nothing because you are confident of your skills and position, besides:
    - It may be a passing phase
    - It may not be worth the energy
    - If you give them enough rope they will probably hang themselves

92

ACHIEVING RESULTS

ACHIEVING RESULTS

WHY IT'S IMPORTANT

Your effectiveness as a manager is often judged on the results that you achieve with the resources under your control. As such remember that:

● You can't do everything yourself; sooner or later you will have to let go and start to trust people

● As a manager, the abilities/results of your staff reflect how well you have trained and managed them

● Planning the work of your section and its people is a key skill

● Plans are ways of turning aims and objectives into actions; remember, they need not be set in concrete. You can always alter them if situations change

PLANS ALWAYS GO WRONG?
SIGNS

You make plans which typically never work:

- What you think/want/hope/expect to happen, often/rarely/never does

- Despite giving yourself plenty of time, you always seem to be rushing around at the end

- You are always talking about:
    - What might have been
    - What you were hoping for

- It's beginning to affect staff:
    - They distrust you (your plans are a joke)
    - There's low morale
    - Productivity and quality decline
    - People go absent

PLANS ALWAYS GO WRONG?
POSSIBLE REASONS

- Poor planning, e.g.:
    - You set unrealistic/over-optimistic targets
    - You or your staff are inexperienced at doing the job

- Unforeseen events, beyond your control

- Pressure of work

- Conflicting priorities

- Failure to consult those who might be affected

- Poor communication or lack of it

    many assumptions made

    bad luck?

ACHIEVING RESULTS

PLANS ALWAYS GO WRONG?

THEN TRY .....

1 Recognising that you **must** have some planning skills, so:
- Think of something you have organised **successfully** (e.g.: an event at work/home, a surprise, a trip, etc)
    - What did you try to do?
    - Why - on reflection - was it a success?
- Then consider something that **did not go well:**
    - Again, what did you try to do?
    - What happened and why?
- From the two, what do you conclude makes a good plan? It could be that:
    - It was well thought out
    - You identified everything you had to do
    - You anticipated what could go wrong and made contingencies
    - It was realistic given the resources and timescales
    - You involved others at every stage

'If I had 9 hours to cut down a tree, I would spend 6 hours sharpening my axe'.
Abraham Lincoln

PLANS ALWAYS GO WRONG?
THEN TRY .....

2 Setting yourself objectives; Remember these must be
   S pecific
   M easureable
   A chievable
   C hallenging
3 Listing your actions:
   - What **exactly** have you got to do?
   - What resources will you need?
   - What are the critical parts of your plan?
   - What could go wrong and why?
   - How might you overcome any problems?
4 Talking to those involved:
   - Get their ideas and commitment
5 Putting the plan into action and:
   - Monitor it at every stage
   - If things aren't going right - or according to plan - then make changes

ACHIEVING RESULTS

STAFF PRODUCE WORK LATE

SIGNS

The people you are relying on to help you never quite come up with the goods when they are needed. For example:

- People always making promises and failing to deliver
- Deadlines are missed and excuses made
- They refuse offers of help
- Panics/crises occur

- You get to the stage where you can't rely on anybody with any confidence
- There's a 'knock-on' effect: late work holds others up who in turn complain to you, etc

'It's a funny thing about life: if you refuse to accept anything but the best, you very often get it.' Somerset Maugham

(99)

STAFF PRODUCE WORK LATE

POSSIBLE REASONS

- They have poor personal organisation skills:
    - Can't prioritise
    - Unable to think in a disciplined manner
    - Not good at planning
- Job is too much for them:
    - Over promoted
    - Out of their depth and don't want to admit it
    - Poor or inadequate training for the job
    - Deadlines are too tight (or too often extended so not taken seriously)
    - Lack of resources
- Bad management on your part:
    - You delegated but possibly failed to monitor progress
    - You allowed situations to develop without taking action sooner
    - Inappropriate delegation (too big a task, too inexperienced a person, etc)

STAFF PRODUCE WORK LATE

THEN TRY .....

- Not blaming the individual(s); try looking at yourself: remember, staff are a reflection of you; you are responsible for their (in)actions

- Getting the facts: is it the first time it's happened or is it a regular occurrence?

- Watching how they work: anything you have spotted that they could do better or differently?

- Talking to them:
    - Face them with the facts
    - Share your observations
    - Ask for their view/explanation
    - Consider what you can **both** do to make sure that it does not happen again (see section on Giving Feedback, Page 21)

STAFF PRODUCE WORK LATE
THEN TRY .....

- Helping them get organised by:
    - Working with them
    - Sharing your experience
    - Involving others if necessary
- Breaking down the jobs that you ask them to do
- To do these jobs:
    - What do they need to **know?**
    - What **skills** are needed?
    - Have they got the right **attitude?** (Remember, changing a person's attitude involves getting them to think and behave differently)
    - Can they perform to the standard you want; if not what can you do to help?
- Making a training plan and monitoring it carefully
- Ensuring that key activities are carried out and essential dates are met

UNEVEN WORKLOAD?
SIGNS

The workload of your section is **either:**
- Very busy:
    - There is a lot of activity
    - Everybody working long hours
    - Rushing around (high energy)
    - 'Time flies'
    - There are not enough hours in the day

or:
- Very quiet:
    - 'Time drags'
    - People clock watch
    - There's low energy and a lot of yawning
    - Staff hunt around for jobs

UNEVEN WORKLOAD?
POSSIBLE REASONS

- It's the nature of the business/job:
    - Key times, such as Christmas, end of financial year or budget time

- Work flow is out of your control:
    - Demand for your 'products' is cyclical
    - It relies on sales people winning orders in a tough market

- Poor planning and work scheduling

The result of all this is that you could be facing a difficult situation:
- If you have long quiet periods, then picking up again may take some time
- How do you keep your people busy/motivated during quiet times?

ACHIEVING RESULTS

UNEVEN WORKLOAD?
THEN TRY .....

- Finding out what causes it:
  - Does it always happen?
  - Can you influence the work flow by explaining to others the implications of what's happening?

- Considering whether you need staff all the time:
  - Can you retain a 'core' of people and bring in staff at busy/peak times?

- Making good use of slack times:
  - Use it for training
  - Do jobs that you were meant to do but were previously too busy to undertake
  - Review your work methods
  - Take on additional work from elsewhere
  - Reduce the working hours when you are less busy

USEFUL READING

Kogan Page has a range of practical books covering many aspects of management, in particular:

'Managing Difficult Staff', an excellent book by Helga Drummond, outlines the legal position and offers case studies together with suggestions to follow.

Fontana/Collins publish a series of books under the heading 'The Successful Manager'.

Sphere have a collection of books under 'Management Handbook' title - easy to follow and well illustrated

BBC BOOKS publish masses of information for managers, much of which links with television/radio series that are running at the time.

'Inside Organisations' by **Charles Handy** offers 21 ideas for managers in his own inimitable, stimulating and readable style

IPM (Institute of Personnel Management) produce many books on a range of people related topics.

Anything by **Peter Honey** is always worth a look. Try 'People Problems and How to Manage Them' as well as 'Improving Your People Skills'

About the Author

Ian Fleming, MA DMS DipEd, works as a freelance management trainer. His approach is to work mainly in-company, helping managers and their teams tackle real problems and opportunities. He has a preference for coaching rather than lecturing.

He is a member of the Focus Consulting Group.

This pocketbook is the product of years of working with managers and the situations they face. This is one of four pocketbooks that he has written, including the well received 'Time Management Pocketbook'.

Should you want to talk to Ian about his ideas and approach, he can be contacted at: 2 Robins Orchard, Chalfont St Peter, Bucks SL9 0HQ. Tel: 01494 873623.

Acknowledgements
To Margaret Manson of Clerical Medical for the concept of 'Appreciating Supervision' and to Pat who has been through it all.

© Copyright Ian Fleming 1993.
Published by Management Pocketbooks 1993   Reprinted 1995, 1997

ISBN 1 870471 16 4

Printed in England by Alresford Press Ltd., Alresford, Hampshire.

ORDER FORM

Your details

Name _____

Position _____

Company _____

Address _____

_____

_____

_____

Telephone _____

Facsimile _____

VAT No. (EC companies) _____

Your Order Ref _____

Please send me:

		No. copies
The _People Manager's_ Pocketbook	☐
The _____ Pocketbook	☐
The _____ Pocketbook	☐
The _____ Pocketbook	☐
The _____ Pocketbook	☐
The _____ Pocketbook	☐
The _____ Pocketbook	☐

MANAGEMENT POCKETBOOKS
14 EAST STREET ALRESFORD
HANTS SO24 9EE UK
Tel: +44 (0)1962 735573
Fax: +44 (0)1962 733637
E-mail: pocketbks@aol.com